The Mersey Sound

ADRIAN HENRI was born at Birkenhead, Cheshire, in 1932. When he was four his family moved to Rhyl, North Wales, where he attended grammar school. From 1950, for ten seasons, he worked in Rhyl fairground, meanwhile studying for a B.A. degree in fine art, which he received from the University of Durham in 1955. He went to live in Liverpool in 1957 and worked as a scenic artist at the Playhouse before holding various teaching jobs. He became interested in poetry performance in 1961, when he first met Roger McGough and Brian Patten. From 1967 to 1970 he led the poetry/rock group 'Liverpool Scene' and was a member of the roadshow 'Grimms' between 1971 and 1973. From 1970 he was a freelance poet/painter/singer/songwriter and lecturer and toured extensively in Europe and elsewhere, including the United States and Canada. His paintings were exhibited widely, including six John Moores Liverpool exhibitions, and he had several one-man shows. He was President of the Liverpool Academy of Arts from 1972 to 1981 and President of the Merseyside Arts Association from 1972 to 1980.

His poetry books include *Tonight at Noon* (1968), *City* (1969), *Autobiography* (1971), *The Best of Henri* (1975), *City Hedges* (1977), *From the Loveless Motel* (1980) and *Penny Arcade* (1983). His poems are included in the anthologies *The Liverpool Scene* (1967), *British Poets of Our Time* (1970) and *The Oxford Book of Twentieth-Century Verse* (1973). Other publications include a novel, *I Want* (with Nell Dunn), *Environment and Happenings* (Thames & Hudson World of Art series, 1974) and a story for children, *Eric the Punk Cat*. Among his plays are *I Wonder* (with Michael Kustow), *Yesterday's Girl* (for Granada television, 1973) and, with Nell Dunn, an adaptation of *I Want* (1983). Adrian Henri died in 2000.

ROGER MCGOUGH was born in Liverpool. He is the author of over fifty books of poetry for both adults and children, as well as editing numerous anthologies. During the 1960's he was part of The Scaffold, whose song 'Lily the Pink' was a hit worldwide. The winner of two Baftas for his film work and a Royal Television Society Award, he helped write the script for *The Yellow Submarine* animation film. A Fellow of the Royal Society of Literature, he has a Cholmondley Award and is twice winner of both the Signal and CLPE Awards for the best book of poetry for children. Much travelled and translated, he is now an international ambassador for poetry, and was made a Freeman of the City of Liverpool in 2001, and received a CBE from the Queen in 2004, for services to literature.

BRIAN PATTEN was born in Liverpool in 1946. His collections of poetry for adults include *Little Johnny's Confession*, *Notes to the Hurrying Man*, *The Irrelevant Song*, *Armada*, and *The Collected Love Poems*, while his collections of verse for children include the bestselling *Gargling With Jelly* and *Juggling With Gerbils*. His novel for children, *Mr Moon's Last Case*, won a special award from The Mystery Writers of America Guild, and his interweaving of international folk and fairy-tales, *The Story Giant*, has been hailed as a modern classic. He is the editor of *The Puffin Book of Modern Verse*. Brian Patten's work has been widely translated. He is a Fellow of the Royal Society of Literature and in 2001 was honoured with the Freedom of the City of Liverpool.

ADRIAN HENRI
ROGER MCGOUGH
BRIAN PATTEN

The Mersey Sound

Revised Edition

PENGUIN BOOKS

PENGUIN BOOKS

Published by the Penguin Group
Penguin Books Ltd, 80 Strand, London WC2R ORL, England
Penguin Group (USA) Inc., 375 Hudson Street, New York, New York 10014, USA
Penguin Group (Canada), 90 Eglinton Avenue East, Suite 700, Toronto, Ontario, Canada M4P 2Y3
(a division of Pearson Penguin Canada Inc.)
Penguin Ireland, 25 St Stephen's Green, Dublin 2, Ireland (a division of Penguin Books Ltd)
Penguin Group (Australia), 250 Camberwell Road, Camberwell, Victoria 3124, Australia
(a division of Pearson Australia Group Pty Ltd)
Penguin Books India Pvt Ltd, 11 Community Centre, Panchsheel Park, New Delhi – 110 017, India
Penguin Group (NZ), 67 Apollo Drive, Rosedale, North Shore 0632, New Zealand
(a division of Pearson New Zealand Ltd)
Penguin Books (South Africa) (Pty) Ltd, 24 Sturdee Avenue,
Rosebank, Johannesburg 2196, South Africa

Penguin Books Ltd, Registered Offices: 80 Strand, London WC2R ORL, England

www.penguin.com

This selection first published 1967
Revised and enlarged edition 1974
Revised edition 1983
Published in Penguin Classics with revisions 2007
7

821 HEN

Set in 10.5/13 pt Monotype Dante
Typeset by Rowland Phototypesetting Ltd, Bury St Edmunds, Suffolk
Printed in Great Britain by Clays Ltd, St Ives plc

ISBN: 978-0-141-18926-0

www.greenpenguin.co.uk

Penguin Books is committed to a sustainable future
for our business, our readers and our planet.
The book in your hands is made from paper
certified by the Forest Stewardship Council.

Contents

Roger McGough

Brian Patten

Acknowledgements

The poems by Adrian Henri are taken from the following books, to whose publishers acknowledgement is due: 'Nightsong', 'Bomb Commercials', 'Who?', 'Batpoem', 'Galactic Lovepoem', 'Love from Arthur Rainbow' from *Tonight at Noon*, 1968, Rapp & Whiting; 'Me', 'The Entry of Christ Into Liverpool', 'The New, Fast, Automatic Daffodils', 'See The Conkering Heroine Comes', 'Short Poems', 'from "City" Part Three', 'Car Crash Blues' from *The Best of Henri*, 1975, Jonathan Cape Ltd. For the rest of the poems acknowledgement is due to the author.

The poems by Roger McGough are taken from the following books, to whose publishers acknowledgement is due: 'My cat and i', 'Snipers', 'My Busconductor', 'Discretion' from *Watchwords*, 1968, Jonathan Cape Ltd; 'Sad Aunt Madge', 'Motorway', 'At Lunchtime', 'Let Me Die a Youngman's Death' from *The Liverpool Scene*, 1967, Donald Carroll; 'Goodbat Nightman' from *In the Glassroom*, 1976, Jonathan Cape Ltd. The rest of the poems were first published by Penguin Books in an earlier edition.

The poems by Brian Patten are taken from the following books, to whose publisher acknowledgement is due: 'Somewhere Between Heaven and Woolworths, A Song', 'Little Johnny's Confession', 'Party Piece', 'A Creature to Tell the Time By', 'Where Are You Now, Batman?', 'A Green Sportscar', 'After Breakfast', 'Song for Last Year's Wife', 'Prosepoem Towards a Definition of Itself', 'Something That Was Not There Before', 'In a New Kind of Dawn', 'On the Dawn Boat', 'Sing Softly', 'Sleep Now', 'Seascape', 'The River Arse', 'Room', 'Come into the City Maud', 'Schoolboy', 'On a Horse Called Autumn', 'The Fruitful Lady of Dawn', 'A Talk with a Wood', 'Travelling Between Places', 'Looking Back at It' from *Little Johnny's Confession*, 1967, George Allen & Unwin Ltd; 'Doubt Shall Not Make an End of You', 'A Small Dragon' from *Notes to the Hurrying Man*, 1969, George Allen & Unwin Ltd; 'Meat', 'The Last

Residents' from *The Irrelevant Song*, 1971, George Allen & Unwin Ltd. The rest of the poems were first published by Penguin Books in an earlier edition.

Note: Some of the poems have been revised since their first publication.

ADRIAN HENRI

Tonight at Noon[*]

(for Charles Mingus and the Clayton Squares)

Tonight at noon
Supermarkets will advertise 3p EXTRA on everything
Tonight at noon
Children from happy families will be sent to live in a home
Elephants will tell each other human jokes
America will declare peace on Russia
World War I generals will sell poppies in the streets on
     November 11th
The first daffodils of autumn will appear
When the leaves fall upwards to the trees

Tonight at noon
Pigeons will hunt cats through city backyards
Hitler will tell us to fight on the beaches and on the landing
     fields
A tunnel full of water will be built under Liverpool
Pigs will be sighted flying in formation over Woolton
and Nelson will not only get his eye back but his arm as well
White Americans will demonstrate for equal rights
in front of the Black House
and the Monster has just created Dr Frankenstein

Girls in bikinis are moonbathing
Folksongs are being sung by real folk
Artgalleries are closed to people over 21
Poets get their poems in the Top 20
Politicians are elected to insane asylums
There's jobs for everyone and nobody wants them
In back alleys everywhere teenage lovers are kissing
in broad daylight

---

[*] The title for this poem is taken from an LP by Charles Mingus, 'Tonight at Noon',
Atlantic 1416.

In forgotten graveyards everywhere the dead will quietly
bury the living
and
You will tell me you love me
Tonight at noon

Mrs Albion You've Got a Lovely Daughter

(for Allen Ginsberg)

Albion's most lovely daughter sat on the banks of the
   Mersey dangling her landing stage in the water.

The daughters of Albion
   arriving by underground at Central Station
   eating hot ecclescakes at the Pierhead
   writing 'Billy Blake is fab' on a wall in Mathew St
   taking off their navyblue schooldrawers and
   putting on nylon panties ready for the night

The daughters of Albion
   see the moonlight beating down on them in Bebington
   throw away their chewinggum ready for the goodnight
      kiss
sleep in the dinnertime sunlight with old men
   looking up their skirts in St Johns Gardens
comb their darkblonde hair in suburban bedrooms
powder their delicate little nipples/wondering if tonight will
      be the night
their bodies pressed into dresses or sweaters
lavender at The Cavern or pink at The Sink

The daughters of Albion
   wondering how to explain why they didn't go home

The daughters of Albion
   taking the dawn ferry to tomorrow
   worrying about what happened
   worrying about what hasn't happened
   lacing up blue sneakers over brown ankles
   fastening up brown stockings to blue suspenderbelts

Beautiful boys with bright red guitars
in the spaces between the stars

Reelin' an' a-rockin'
Wishin' an' a-hopin'
Kissin' an' a-prayin'
Lovin' an' a-layin'

Mrs Albion you've got a lovely daughter.

Adrian Henri's Talking After Christmas Blues

Well I woke up this mornin' it was Christmas Day
And the birds were singing the night away
I saw my stocking lying on the chair
Looked right to the bottom but you weren't there
there was
      apples
        oranges
          chocolates
            . . . aftershave
– but no you.

So I went downstairs and the dinner was fine
There was pudding and turkey and lots of wine
And I pulled those crackers with a laughing face
Till I saw there was no one in your place
there was
      mincepies
        brandy
          nuts and raisins
            . . . mashed potato
– but no you.

Now it's New Year and it's Auld Lang Syne
And it's 12 o'clock and I'm feeling fine
Should Auld Acquaintance be Forgot?
I don't know girl, but it hurts a lot
there was
      whisky
        vodka
          dry Martini (stirred but not shaken)
            . . . and 12 New Year resolutions
– all of them about you.

So it's all the best for the year ahead
As I stagger upstairs and into bed
Then I looked at the pillow by my side
. . . I tell you baby I almost cried
there'll be

        Autumn

          Summer

            Spring

              . . . and Winter

– all of them without you.

In the Midnight Hour

When we meet
in the midnight hour
country girl
I will bring you nightflowers
coloured like your eyes
in the moonlight
in the midnight
hour

I remember

Your cold hand
held for a moment among strangers
held for a moment among dripping trees
in the midnight hour

I remember

Your eyes coloured like the autumn landscape
walking down muddy lanes
watching sheep eating yellow roses
walking in city squares in winter rain
kissing in darkened hallways
walking in empty suburban streets
saying goodnight in deserted alleyways

in the midnight hour

Andy Williams singing 'We'll keep a Welcome in the
    Hillsides' for us
When I meet you at the station
The Beatles singing 'We Can Work it Out' with James Ensor
    at the harmonium
Rita Hayworth in a nightclub singing 'Amade Mia'

I will send you armadas
of love vast argosies of flowers
in the midnight hour
country girl

when we meet

in the
moonlight
midnight
hour
country girl

I will bring you

yellow
white
eyes
bright
moon
light
mid
night
flowers
in the midnight hour.

Love Is . . .

Love is feeling cold in the back of vans
Love is a fanclub with only two fans
Love is walking holding paintstained hands
Love is

Love is fish and chips on winter nights
Love is blankets full of strange delights
Love is when you don't put out the light
Love is

Love is the presents in Christmas shops
Love is when you're feeling Top of the Pops
Love is what happens when the music stops
Love is

Love is white panties lying all forlorn
Love is a pink nightdress still slightly warm
Love is when you have to leave at dawn
Love is

Love is you and love is me
Love is a prison and love is free
Love's what's there when you're away from me
Love is . . .

The New 'Our Times'

(for Félix Fénéon)*

I

At 3 p.m. yesterday, a Mr Adolphus Edwards, a Jamaican immigrant, was pecked to death by a large Bronze Eagle in Upper Parliament St. A U.S. State Dept. spokesman said later, 'We have no comment to make as of this time.'

2

Police-Constable George Williams, who was partially blinded by a 15 lb jellybaby thrown at a passing pop singer, is to be retired on half-pension.

3

Bearded Liverpool couple put out of misery in night by drip oil heater, court told.

4

A certain Mrs Elspeth Clout, of Huyton, was killed by an unidentified falling object. It was thought to be a particularly hard stool evacuated from the toilet of a passing aeroplane.

* (A free 1960s Liverpool version of Fénéon's great 'Our Times'.)

5

2 chip-shop proprietors were today accused of selling human ears fried in batter. One of them said 'We believe there is room for innovation in the trade.'

6

Fatality in Kardomah bomb outrage: Waitress buried Alive under two thousand Danish pastries.

7

At the inquest on Paul McCartney, aged 21, described as a popular singer and guitarist, P.C. Smith said, in evidence, that he saw one of the accused, Miss Jones, standing waving blood-stained hands shouting 'I got a bit of his liver.'

I Want To Paint

Part One

I want to paint
2000 dead birds crucified on a background of night
Thoughts that lie too deep for tears
Thoughts that lie too deep for queers
Thoughts that move at 186000 miles/second
The Entry of Christ into Liverpool in 1966
The Installation of Roger McGough to the Chair of Poetry at
    Oxford
Francis Bacon making the President's Speech at the Royal
    Academy Dinner

I want to paint
50 life-sized nudes of Marianne Faithfull
(all of them painted from life)
Welsh Maids by Welsh Waterfalls
Heather Holden as Our Lady of Haslingden
A painting as big as Piccadilly full of neon signs buses
Christmas decorations and beautiful girls with dark blonde
    hair shading their faces

I want to paint
The assassination of the entire Royal Family
Enormous pictures of every pavingstone in Canning Street
The Beatles composing a new National Anthem
Brian Patten writing poems with a flamethrower on disused
    ferryboats

A new cathedral 50 miles high made entirely of pram-wheels
An empty Woodbine packet covered in kisses
I want to paint
A picture made from the tears of dirty-faced children in
    Chatham Street
I want to paint
I LOVE YOU across the steps of St George's Hall
I want to paint
        pictures.

Part Two

I want to paint
The Simultaneous and Historical Faces of Death
10000 shocking pink hearts with your name on
The phantom negro postmen who bring me money in my
    dreams
The first plastic daffodil of Spring pushing its way
through the OMO packets in the Supermarket
The portrait of every 6th Form schoolgirl in the country
A full-scale map of the World with YOU at the centre
An enormous lily-of-the-valley with every flower on a
    separate canvas

Lifesize jellybabies shaped like Hayley Mills
A black-and-red flag flying over Parliament
I want to paint
Every car crash on all the motorways of England
Père Ubu drunk at 11 o'clock at night in Lime Street
A SYSTEMATIC DERANGEMENT OF ALL THE SENSES
In black running letters 50 miles high over Liverpool

I want to paint
Pictures that children can play hopscotch on
Pictures that can be used as evidence at Murder trials
Pictures that can be used to advertise cornflakes
Pictures that can be used to frighten naughty children
Pictures worth their weight in money

Pictures that tramps can live in
Pictures that children would find in their stockings on
     Christmas morning
Pictures that teenage lovers can send each other
I want to paint
                    pictures.

Adrian Henri's Last Will and Testament

'No one owns life, but anyone who can pick up a fryingpan owns death.'
  William Burroughs

To whom it may concern:
As my imminent death is hourly expected these days/
carbrakes screaming on East Lancs tarmac/trapped
in the blazing cinema/mutely screaming I TOLD YOU SO
from melting eyeballs as the whitehot fireball
dissolves the Cathedral/being the first human being to die
of a hangover/dying of over-emotion after seeing 20
schoolgirls waiting at a zebracrossing.

I appoint Messrs Bakunin and Kropotkin my executors
and make the following provisions:

1. I leave my priceless collections of Victorian Oil Lamps,
photographs of Hayley Mills, brass fenders and Charlie
Mingus records to all Liverpool poets under 23 who are
also blues singers and failed sociology students.

2. I leave the entire East Lancs Road with all its landscapes
to the British people.

3. I hereby appoint Wm. Burroughs my literary executor,
instructing him to cut up my collected works and
distribute them through the public lavatories of the world.

4. Proceeds from the sale of relics: locks of hair, pieces
of floorboards I have stood on, fragments of bone flesh
teeth bits of old underwear etc. to be given to my widow.

5. I leave my paintings to the Nation with the stipulation that they must be exhibited in Public Houses, Chip Shops, Coffee Bars and the Cellar Clubs throughout the country.

6. Proceeds from the sale of my other effects to be divided equally amongst the 20 most beautiful schoolgirls in England (these to be chosen after due deliberation and exhaustive tests by an informal committee of my friends).

Adrian Henri
Jan. '64

Witnessed this day by
James Ensor
Charlie 'Bird' Parker

Without You

Without you every morning would be like going back to
    work after a holiday,
Without you I couldn't stand the smell of the East Lancs
    Road,
Without you ghost ferries would cross the Mersey manned
    by skeleton crews,
Without you I'd probably feel happy and have more money
    and time and nothing to do with it,
Without you I'd have to leave my stillborn poems on other
    people's doorsteps, wrapped in brown paper,
Without you there'd never be sauce to put on sausage
    butties,
Without you plastic flowers in shop windows would just be
    plastic flowers in shop windows
Without you I'd spend my summers picking morosely over
    the remains of train crashes,
Without you white birds would wrench themselves free from
    my paintings and fly off dripping blood into the night,
Without you green apples wouldn't taste greener,
Without you Mothers wouldn't let their children play out
    after tea,
Without you every musician in the world would forget how
    to play the blues,
Without you Public Houses would be public again,
Without you the Sunday Times colour supplement would
    come out in black-and-white,
Without you indifferent colonels would shrug their shoulders
    and press the button,
Without you they'd stop changing the flowers in Piccadilly
    Gardens,
Without you Clark Kent would forget how to become
    Superman,

Without you Sunshine Breakfast would only consist of
    Cornflakes,
Without you there'd be no colour in Magic colouring books
Without you Mahler's 8th would only be performed by street
    musicians in derelict houses,
Without you they'd forget to put the salt in every packet of
    crisps,
Without you it would be an offence punishable by a fine of
    up to £200 or two months imprisonment to be found in
    possession of curry powder,
Without you riot police are massing in quiet sidestreets,
Without you all streets would be one-way the other way,
Without you there'd be no one not to kiss goodnight when
    we quarrel,
Without you the first martian to land would turn round and
    go away again,
Without you they'd forget to change the weather,
Without you blind men would sell unlucky heather,
Without you there would be
no landscapes/no stations/no houses,
no chipshops/no quiet villages/no seagulls
on beaches/no hopscotch on pavements/no
night/no morning/there'd be no city no country
Without you.

Liverpool Poems

I

GO TO WORK ON A BRAQUE!

2

Youths disguised as stockbrokers
Sitting on the grass eating the Sacred Mushroom.

3

Liverpool I love your horny-handed tons of soil.

4

PRAYER FROM A PAINTER TO ALL CAPITALISTS:
   Open your wallets and repeat after me
     'HELP YOURSELF!'

5

There's one way of being sure of keeping fresh
LIFEBUOY helps you rise again on the 3rd day
after smelling something that smelt like other people's socks.

6

Note for a definition of optimism:
A man trying the door of Yates Wine Lodge
At quarter past four in the afternoon.

7

I have seen Père UBU walking across Lime St
And Alfred Jarry cycling down Elliott Street.

8

And I saw DEATH in Upper Duke St
Cloak flapping black tall Batman collar
Striding tall shoulders down the hill past the Cathedral
   brown shoes slightly down at the heel.

9

Unfrocked Chinese mandarins holding lonely feasts in
      Falkner Sq gardens
to enjoy the snow.

10

Prostitutes in the snow in Canning St like strange erotic
      snowmen
And Marcel Proust in the Kardomah eating Madeleine butties
      dipped in tea.

11

Wyatt James Virgil and Morgan Earp with Doc Holliday
Shooting it out with the Liver Birds at the Pier Head.

12

And a Polish gunman young beautiful dark glasses
combatjacket/staggers down Little St Bride St blood
dripping moaning clutches/collapses down a back jigger
coughing/falls in a wilderness of Dazwhite washing.

Nightsong

So we'll go no more a-raving
So late into the night
Though the heart be still as loving
And the neonsigns so bright

Ate my breakfast egg this morning
playing records from last night
woke to hear the front door closing
as the sky was getting light

No more fish-and-chips on corners
watching traffic going by
No more branches under streetlamps
No more leaves against the sky

No more blues by Otis Redding
No more coffee no more bread
No more dufflecoats for bedding
No more cushions for your head

Though the night is daylight-saving
And the day returns too soon
Still we'll go no more a-raving
By the light of the moon

Bomb Commercials

(for two voices)

1 A.   Get PAD nuclear meat for humans
   B.   Don't give your family ordinary meat, give them PAD
   A.   P.A.D. – Prolongs Active Death
   B.   Enriched with nourishing marrowbone strontium.

2 A.   All over the world, more and more people are changing
        to

                            BOMB
   B.   BOMB – The International passport to smoking ruins

3 B.   . . . so then I said 'well lets all go for a picnic and we went and
        it was all right except for a bit of sand in the butties and then of
        course the wasps and Michael fell in the river but what I say is
        you can't have everything perfect can you so just then there was
        a big bang and the whole place caught fire and something hap-
        pened to Michael's arms and I don't know what happened to
        my Hubby and its perhaps as well as there were only four pieces
        of Kit-Kat so we had one each and then we had to walk home
        'cos there weren't any buses . . .
   A.   HAVE A BREAK – HAVE A KIT-KAT

4 A.   Everyday in cities all over England people are breathing
        in Fall-out
   B.   Get the taste of the Bomb out of your mouth with OVAL
        FRUITS

5 A.   General Howard J. Sherman has just pressed the button
        that killed 200 million people. A BIG job with BIG respon-
        sibilities. The General has to decide between peace and
        the extinction of the human race . . .
   B.   But he can't tell Stork from Butter.

Who?

Who can I
spend my life
with
Who can I
listen to Georges Brassens
singing
'Les amoureux des bancs publiques'
with
Who can I
go to Paris with
getting drunk at night with
tall welldressed spades
Who can I
quarrel with
outside chipshops
in sidestreets
on landings
Who else
can sing along with Shostakovitch
Who else
would sign a Christmas card
'Cannonball'
Who else
can work the bathroom geyser
Who else
drinks as much bitter
Who else
makes all my favourite meals
except the ones I make
myself
Who else
would bark back at dogs

in the moonlit lamplit streets
Who else
would I find
waiting dark bigeyed
in a corner of a provincial jazzclub
You say
we don't get on
anymore
but
who can I
laugh on beaches with
wondering at the noise
the limpets make
still sucking in the tide
Who
can I
buy
my next Miles Davis record
to share with
who
makes coffee the way I like it
and
love the way I used to like it
who
came in from the sun
the day
the world went spinning away
from me
who
doesn't wash the clothes I always want
who
spends my money
who
wears my dressing gown
and always leaves the sleeves turned up
who
makes me feel
as empty as the house does

when she's not there
who
else
but
you

for Joyce

Batpoem

(for Bob Kane and The Almost Blues)

Take me back to Gotham City
   Batman
Take me where the girls are pretty
   Batman

All those damsels in distress
Half-undressed or even less
The BatPill makes 'em all say Yes
   Batman

Help us out in Vietnam
   Batman
Help us drop that BatNapalm
   Batman

Help us bomb those jungle towns
Spreading pain and death around
Coke 'n' Candy wins them round
   Batman

Help us smash the Vietcong
   Batman
Help us show them that they're wrong
   Batman

Help us spread Democracy
Get them high on L.S.D.
Make them just like you and me
   Batman
Show me what I have to do
   Batman
'Cause I want to be like you
   Batman

Flash your Batsign over Lime Street
Batmobiles down every crimestreet
Happy Batday that's when I'll meet
          Batman

Galactic Lovepoem

(for Susan)

Warm your feet at the sunset
Before we go to bed
Read your book by the light of Orion
With Sirius guarding your head
Then reach out and switch off the planets
We'll watch them go out one by one
You kiss me and tell me you love me
By the light of the last setting sun
We'll both be up early tomorrow
A new universe has begun

Love From Arthur Rainbow

In a villa called 'Much Bickering'
In a street called Pleasant Street
Living with her wicked parents
Was a princess, small and neat

She wanted to be an artist
So off to a college she went
And as long as she got a Diploma
They considered it money well spent

One day she met a poet
Who taught her all about life
He walked her down to the station
Then went back home to his wife

He came from the end of the rainbow
At least that's what she thought
The kind of love she wanted
The kind that can't be bought

But time and the last train to the suburbs
Killed the love that would never die
And he'll find another lover
And she'll sit at home and cry

Now she's reading through his letters
In her small schoolteacher flat
Dusty paint-tubes in the corner
Worn-out 'Welcome' on the mat

O the day she met Arthur Rainbow
There were roses all over town
There were angels in all the shopwindows
And kisses not rain coming down

Now it's off to work every morning
And back home for dinner at eight
For the gold at the end of the rainbow
Lies buried beneath her front gate.

Me

if you weren't you, who would you like to be?

Paul McCartney Gustav Mahler
Alfred Jarry John Coltrane
Charlie Mingus Claude Debussy
Wordsworth Monet Bach and Blake

Charlie Parker Pierre Bonnard
Leonardo Bessie Smith
Fidel Castro Jackson Pollock
Gaudi Milton Munch and Berg

Béla Bartók Henri Rousseau
Rauschenberg and Jasper Johns
Lukas Cranach Shostakovich
Kropotkin Ringo George and John

William Burroughs Francis Bacon
Dylan Thomas Luther King
H.P. Lovecraft T.S. Eliot
D.H. Lawrence Roland Kirk

Salvatore Giuliano
Andy Warhol Paul Cézanne
Kafka Camus Ensor Rothko
Jacques Prévert and Manfred Mann

Marx Dostoievsky
Bakunin Ray Bradbury
Miles Davis Trotsky
Stravinsky and Poe

Danilo Dolci Napoleon Solo
St John of the Cross and
The Marquis de Sade

Charles Rennie Mackintosh
Rimbaud Claes Oldenburg
Adrian Mitchell and Marcel Duchamp

James Joyce and Hemingway
Hitchcock and Buñuel
Donald McKinlay Thelonius Monk

Alfred, Lord Tennyson
Matthias Grünewald
Philip Jones Griffiths and Roger McGough

Guillaume Apollinaire
Cannonball Adderley
René Magritte
Hieronymus Bosch

Stéphane Mallarmé and Alfred de Vigny
Ernst Mayakovsky and Nicolas de Staël
Hindemith Mick Jagger Dürer and Schwitters
Garcia Lorca
                    and
                         last of all
                                   me.

The Entry of Christ Into Liverpool

City morning, dandelionseeds blowing from wasteground.
smell of overgrown privethedges, children's voices
in the distance. sounds from the river.
round the corner into Myrtle St. Saturdaymorning shoppers
headscarves, shoppingbaskets, dogs.

then
  down the hill

THE SOUND OF TRUMPETS
cheering and shouting in the distance
children running
icecream vans
flags breaking out over buildings
black and red green and yellow
Union Jacks Red Ensigns
LONG LIVE SOCIALISM
stretched against the blue sky
over St George's hall

Now the procession

THE MARCHING DRUMS
hideous masked Breughel faces of old ladies in the crowd
yellow masks of girls in curlers and headscarves
smelling of factories
Masks Masks Masks
red masks purple masks pink masks

crushing surging carrying me along
down the hill past the Philharmonic The Labour Exchange
excited feet crushing the geraniums in St Luke's Gardens
placards banners posters

Keep Britain White
End the War in Vietnam
God Bless Our Pope
Billboards hoardings drawings on pavements
words painted on the road
STOP GO HALT
the sounds of pipes and drums down the street
little girls in yellow and orange dresses paper flowers
embroidered banners
Loyal Sons of King William Lodge, Bootle
Masks more Masks crowding in off buses
standing on walls climbing fences

familiar faces among the crowd
faces of my friends the shades of Pierre Bonnard and
Guillaume Apollinaire
Jarry cycling carefully through the crowd. A black cat
picking her way underfoot
posters
signs
gleaming salads
COLMANS MUSTARD
J. Ensor, Fabriqueur de Masques
HAIL JESUS, KING OF THE JEWS
straining forward to catch a glimpse through the crowd
red hair white robe grey donkey
familiar face
trafficlights zebracrossings
GUIN
GUINN
GUINNESS IS

white bird dying unnoticed in a corner
splattered feathers
blood running merged with the neonsigns
in a puddle
GUINNESS IS GOOD
GUINNESS IS GOOD FOR
Masks Masks Masks Masks Masks

GUINNESS IS GOOD FOR YOU
brassbands cheering loudspeakers blaring
clatter of police horses
ALL POWER TO THE CONSTITUENT
ASSEMBLY
masks cheering glittering teeth
daffodils trodden underfoot

BUTCHERS OF JERUSALEM
banners cheering drunks stumbling and singing
masks
masks
masks

evening
thin sickle moon
pale blue sky
flecked with bright orange clouds
streamers newspapers discarded paper hats
blown slowly back up the hill by the evening wind
dustmen with big brooms sweeping the gutters
last of the crowds waiting at bus-stops
giggling schoolgirls quiet businessmen
me
walking home
empty chip-papers drifting round my feet.

The New, Fast, Automatic Daffodils*

(New variation on Wordsworth's 'Daffodils')

I wandered lonely as
THE NEW, FAST DAFFODIL
   FULLY AUTOMATIC
that floats on high o'er vales and hills
The Daffodil is generously dimensioned to accommodate four
                              adult passengers

10,000 saw I at a glance
Nodding their new anatomically shaped heads in sprightly
                              dance

Beside the lake beneath the trees
   in three bright modern colours
red, blue and pigskin
The Daffodil de luxe is equipped with a host of useful
                              accessories
including windscreen wiper and washer with joint control
A Daffodil doubles the enjoyment of touring at home or
                              abroad

in vacant or in pensive mood
SPECIFICATION:
   Overall width   1·44 m (57")
   Overall height   1·38 m (54·3")
   Max. speed   105 km/hr (65 m.p.h.)
     (also cruising speed)
DAFFODIL
   RELIABLE — ECONOMICAL
DAFFODIL
   THE BLISS OF SOLITUDE
DAFFODIL
   The Variomatic Inward Eye
Travelling by Daffodil you can relax and enjoy every mile of
                              the journey.

* (Cut-up of Wordsworth's poem plus Dutch motor-car leaflet)

See The Conkering Heroine Comes

Thinking about you
Walking the woods in Autumn
jumping for branches picking glossy horse-chestnuts from the
ground
caught purple-handed coming back from blackberrying
Walking handinhand in the summer park
flowers dropping on you as we walk through the palm-
house.
magenta to pink to faded rose
pink hearts floating on tiny waterfalls
the woods echoing to the song of the Mersey Bowmen
leaves you said were the colour of the green sweets in
Mackintosh's Weekend
cheeks warm and smooth like peaches not apples
hair caught golden in the sunlight
your child's eyes wondering at the colour of rhododendrons
and the whiteness of swans.

Coming back in Autumn
the air loud with the colours of Saturdayafternoon football
the alleyway of trees they planted for us in summer
still there
young appletrees going to sleep in their applepie beds
tropical plants in the palmhouse you said
looked like lions sticking their tongues out
one faded pink flower left
leaves falling very slowly in the tropical afternoon inside
you suddenly seeing a family of mice
living high up in the painted wroughtiron girders.

Walking back
the lakes cold the rhododendrons shivering slightly in the
                                        dusk
peacocks closing up their tails 'til next summer
your hand in mine
the first frost of winter touching your cheeks.

Short Poems

Love Poem/Colour Supplement

It was our first great war
And after the first successful sortie
Into the nomansgland
between her thighs
We waited anxiously every month
for poppysellers to appear in her streets.

Drinking Song

He became more and more drunk
As the afternoon wore off.

Song for a Beautiful Girl Petrol-Pump Attendant on the Motorway

I wanted your soft verges
But you gave me the hard shoulder.

Poem for Roger McGough

A nun in a Supermarket
Standing in the queue
Wondering what it's like
To buy groceries for two.

Morning Poem

(for Deirdre)
'I've just about reached breaking point'
he snapped.

Love Poem

(for Sydney Hoddes)
'I love you' he said
With his tongue in her cheek.

Buttons

Perhaps you don't love me at all,
but at least you sew buttons on my coat
which is more than my wife does.

Cat Poem

You're black and sleek and beautiful
What a pity your best friends won't tell you
Your breath smells of Kit-E-Kat.

Poem in Memoriam T. S. Eliot

I'd been out the night before & hadn't seen the papers or
    the telly
& the next day in a café someone told me you were dead
And it was as if a favourite distant uncle had died
old hands in the bigstrange room/new shiny presents at
    Christmas
and I didn't know what to feel.

For years I measured out my life with your coffeespoons

Your poems on the table in dusty bedsitters
Playing an L.P. of you reading on wet interrupted January
    afternoons

Meanwhile, back at the Wasteland:
Maureen O'Hara in a lowcut dress staggers across Rhyl
    sandhills
Lovers in Liverpool pubs eating passionfruit
Reading Alfred de Vigny in the lavatory
Opening an old grand piano and finding it smelling of curry
THE STAR OF INDIA FOUND IN A BUS STATION
Making love in a darkened room hearing an old woman
    having a fit on the landing
The first snowflakes of winter falling on her Christmas poem
    for me in Piccadilly Gardens
The first signs of spring in plastic daffodils
on city counters.

Lovers kissing
Rain falling
Dogs running
Night falling

And you 'familiar compound spirit' moving silently down
     Canning St in a night of rain and fog.

Where'er You Walk

'Where'er you walk
Cool gales shall fan that glade'

The Pierhead where you walked will be made a park
restricted to lovers under 21
Peasants will be found merrymaking after the storm in
    Canning St
where you walked
The station where we first arrived at night
Will be preserved for the nation
With the echo of your footsteps still sounding in the empty
    roof

'Where'er you tread
The Blushing flower shall rise'

The alleyway where we read poems to dustbins
after closing time
The kitchens where we quarrelled at parties
The kitchen where two strangers first kissed at a party
full of strangers
The ticketbarrier where we said goodnight so many times
The cobblestones in front of the station
The pub where the kindly old waiter
Always knows what we want to drink –
ALL SHALL BURST INTO BLOOM
SPROUTING FLOWERS BRIGHTER THAN PLASTIC ONES IN
    WOOLWORTHS
Daffodils and chrysanthemums, rhododendrons and
    snowdrops, tulips and roses
– cobblestones bursting with lilies-of-the-valley

'And all things flourish'
Whole streets where you walk are paved with soft grass
so the rain will never go through your shoes again
Zebracrossings made of lilies
Belishabeacons made of orangeblossom
Busstops huge irises
Trafficlights made of snapdragons

'Trees where you sit
Shall crowd into a shade'

even in Piccadilly
stations covered in flowers yellow like the paint you once got
        in your hair
Oaktrees growing everywhere we've kissed
Will still be there when I've forgotten what you look like
And you don't remember me at all
Copies of your letters to me on blue paper
Written on the sky by an aeroplane over all the cities of
        england
Copies of your poems stamped on eggs instead of lions
We will walk forever in the darkness under fernleaves

'Trees where you sit
shall crowd into a shade'

Car Crash Blues or Old Adrian Henri's Interminable Talking Surrealistic Blues

(for Jim Dine and Ch. Baudelaire)

You make me feel like
someone's driven me into a wall
baby
You make me feel like
Sunday night at the village hall
baby
You make me feel like a Desert Rat
You make me feel like a Postman's hat
You make me feel like I've been swept under the mat
baby

You make me feel like
something from beyond the grave
baby
You make me feel like
Woolworths After-Shave
baby
You make me feel like a drunken nun
You make me feel like the war's begun
You make me feel like I'm being underdone
baby

You make me feel like
a Wellington filled with blood
baby
You make me feel like
my clothes are made of wood
baby
You make me feel like a Green Shield stamp
You make me feel like an army camp
You make me feel like a bad attack of cramp
baby

You make me feel like
a limestone quarry
baby
You make me feel like
a Corporation lorry
baby
You make me feel like a hideous sore
You make me feel like a hardware store
You make me feel like something spilt on the floor
baby
You make me feel like
a used Elastoplast
baby
You make me feel like
a broken plastercast
baby
You make me feel like an empty lift
You make me feel like a worthless gift
You make me feel like a slagheap shifting
baby

You make me feel like
last week's knickers
baby
You make me feel like
2 consenting vicars
baby
You make me feel like an overgrown garden
You make me feel like a traffic warden
You make me feel like General Gordon
baby
like a hunchback's hump
like a petrol pump
like the girl
                on the ledge
                            that's afraid to jump
like a
        garbage truck
                    with a heavy load on
                                        baby

Spring Song for Mary

'Lovers twain that cannot wed,
Praising much the greenwood bough,
Where our love may shelter now,
Praising all the leaves that shade us,
Praising, Praising, love that made us . . .'
    Dafydd ap Gwilym, 'The Nightingale in the Birch-Thicket'

echoing birdsong in the dark morning
nightingale from the
birch-thickets of childhood
waking me
distant cuckoofilled woods
in the city lamplight dawn
outside my window

February sunlight slants across swollen fields flooded
        streams
remembering the smell of your hair tangled against lilac
        sheets
Smoke from chimneystacks frozen in the sky
remembering summer thighs under your thin white dress
Sky reflected in lorrytracks through muddy buildingsites
neonsigns reflected in your eyes when we kissed in a taxi
Tiny flecks of rain on the window
young body pale in the autumn evening
Riverbanks bursting
warm mouth shining white teeth
Waves flowing across ploughed fields
my hands under your dress finding you suddenly needing
        me

rain moulting grey from
clouds hanging ragged from

the horizon
empty morning beaches
the silence inside ancient castles
suddenly remembering
running laughing with my friends in the summer wood
writing your name and mine
on a huge oak tree in soft crumbling chalk
train rattling my pen as I write
light birchtrees against sullen woods
wind changing the sea from blue to green
like your eyes
barges drifting on quiet canals

Come close and say the world's at an end
and me with you
There's no tomorrow, just today
Yes, come closer

tall
pylons
into the melting
afternoon
no
blue
envelope
in the morning
hallway
climbing
the abbey steps
near
where you slept
last night
coffee stained
tablecloths
on trains
cries
of seagulls
in your seablue
eyes

small
houses
huddle the hills
from
colliery valleys
warm
touch
of your mouth
in the secret kitchen
bright
bridgelights
in the echoing
Severn
night

'Grant us a day my love and me,
Now love's in blossom on every tree'
   – Dafydd ap Gwilym

Sitting on a train
Wondering will daffodils and rhododendrons stand against
     the cruel bayonets
Will telling my love for you change the Universe?
Will telling you walking to school in winter morning
     darkness
cold in your brown uniform
Keep the Napalm from one frightened child?
Will telling the feel of you under my hands
bring back to life the murdered poet?

Can the thin branches stop the melting snow flooding the
     rivers?
Can my poems become food for the starving of Africa and
     Asia?
Can fieldmice and birdsnests survive the mighty
     earthmovers?
Foxes and badgers, thrushes and nightingales
take back the countryside?
Gleaming fish swim up our polluted rivers again?

Only take this song
As the factories break the skyline
As the overhead wires sing for us
As the skidding motorway tyres
scream your name with their last breath
As the evening snowlight falls on a city street
My pen tracing these words on thin yellow paper

Take
this song.

ROGER McGOUGH

Comeclose and Sleepnow

it is afterwards
and you talk on tiptoe
happy to be part
of the darkness
lips becoming limp
a prelude to tiredness.
Comeclose and Sleepnow
for in the morning
when a policeman
disguised as the sun
creeps into the room
and your mother
disguised as birds
calls from the trees
you will put on a dress of guilt
and shoes with broken high ideals
and refusing coffee
run
alltheway
home.

Aren't We All

Looks quite pretty lying there
Can't be asleep yet
Wonder what she's thinking about?
Penny for her thoughts
Probably not worth it.
There's the moon trying to look romantic
Moon's too old that's her trouble
Aren't we all?

Lace curtains gently swaying
Like a woman walking
A woman in a negligee
Walking out through the window
Over the sleeping city up into the sky
To give the moon a rest
Moon's too tired that's her trouble
Aren't we all?

Wasn't a bad party really
Except for the people
People always spoil things
Room's in a mess
And this one's left her clothes allover the place
Scattered like seeds
In too much of a hurry that's her trouble
Aren't we all?

Think she's asleep now
It makes you sleep
Better than Horlicks
Not so pretty really when you get close-up
Wonder what her name is?
Now she's taken all the blankets
Too selfish that's her trouble
Aren't we all?

A Lot of Water has Flown under your Bridge

i remember your hands
white and strangely cold
asif exposed too often to the moon

i remember your eyes
brown and strangely old
asif exposed too often and too soon

i remember your body
young and strangely bold
asif exposed too often

i remember
i remember how
when you laughed
hotdogmen allover town
burst into song

i remember
i remember how
when you cried
the clouds cried too and the
streets became awash with tears

i remember
i remember how
when we lay together for the first time
the room smiled,
said: 'excuse me',
and tiptoed away.

but time has passed since then
and alotof people
have crossed over the bridge
(a faceless throng)
but time has passed since then
and alotof youngmen
have swum in the water
(naked and strong)

but time has passed since then
and alotof water
   has flown
      under
         your
            bridge.

My cat and i

Girls are simply the prettiest things
My cat and i believe
And we're always saddened
When it's time for them to leave

We watch them titivating
(that often takes a while)
And though they keep us waiting
My cat & i just smile

We like to see them to the door
Say how sad it couldn't last
Then my cat and i go back inside
And talk about the past.

On Picnics

at the goingdown of the sun
and in the morning
i try to remember them
but their names are ordinary names
and their causes are thighbones
tugged excitedly from the soil
by frenchchildren
on picnics

A Square Dance

In Flanders fields in Northern France
They're all doing a brand new dance
It makes you happy and out of breath
And it's called the Dance of Death

Everybody stands in line
Everybody's feeling fine
We're all going to a hop
1 – 2 – 3 and over the top

It's the dance designed to thrill
It's the mustard gas quadrille
A dance for men – girls have no say in it
For your partner is a bayonet

See how the dancers sway and run
To the rhythm of the gun
Swing your partner dos-y-doed
All around the shells explode

Honour your partner form a square
Smell the burning in the air
Over the barbed wire kicking high
Men like shirts hung out to dry

If you fall that's no disgrace
Someone else will take your place
'Old soldiers never die . . .'
                              . . . Only young ones

In Flanders fields where mortars blaze
They're all doing the latest craze
Khaki dancers out of breath
Doing the glorious Dance of Death
Doing the glorious Dance of Death.

Snipers

When I was kneehigh to a tabletop,
Uncle Tom came home from Burma.
He was the youngest of seven brothers
so the street borrowed extra bunting
and whitewashed him a welcome.

All the relations made the pilgrimage,
including us, laughed, sang, made a fuss.
He was as brown as a chairleg,
drank tea out of a white mug the size of my head,
and said next to nowt.

But every few minutes he would scan
the ceiling nervously, hands begin to shake.
'For snipers,' everyone later agreed,
'A difficult habit to break.'

Sometimes when the two of us were alone,
he'd have a snooze after dinner
and I'd keep an eye open for Japs.
Of course he didn't know this
and the tanner he'd give me before I went
was for keeping quiet,
but I liked to think it was money well spent.

Being Uncle Tom's secret bodyguard
had its advantages, the pay was good
and the hours were short, but even so,
the novelty soon wore off, and instead,
I started school and became an infant.

Later, I learned that he was in a mental home.
'Needn't tell anybody . . . Nothing serious
. . . Delayed shock . . . Usual sort of thing
. . . Completely cured now the doctors say.'
The snipers came down from the ceiling
but they didn't go away.

Over the next five years they picked off
three of his brothers; one of whom was my father.
No glory, no citations,
Bang! straight through the heart.

Uncle Tom's married now, with a family.
He doesn't say much, but each night after tea,
he still dozes fitfully in his favourite armchair,
(dreams by courtesy of Henri Rousseau).
He keeps out of the sun, and listens now and then
for the tramp tramp tramp of the Colonel Bogeymen.
He knows damn well he's still at war,
just that the snipers aren't Japs anymore.

Sad Aunt Madge

As the cold winter evenings drew near
Aunt Madge used to put extra blankets
over the furniture, to keep it warm and cosy.
Mussolini was her lover, and life
was an outoffocus rosy-tinted spectacle.

but neurological experts
with kind blueeyes
and gentle voices
small white hands
and large Rolls Royces
said that electric shock treatment
should do the trick
it did . . .

today after 15 years of therapeutic tears
and an awful lot of ratepayers' shillings
down the hospital meter
sad Aunt Madge
no longer tucks up the furniture
before kissing it goodnight
and admits
that her affair with Mussolini
clearly was not right
particularly in the light
of her recently announced engagement
to the late pope.

The Fallen Birdman

The oldman in the cripplechair
Died in transit through the air
And slopped into the road.

The driver of the lethallorry
Trembled out and cried: 'I'm sorry,
But it was his own fault'.

Humans snuggled round the mess
In masochistic tenderness
As raindrops danced in his womb.

*   *   *

But something else obsessed my brain,
The canvas, twistedsteel and cane,
His chair, spreadeagled in the rain,
Like a fallen birdman.

The Icingbus

the littleman
with the hunchbackedback
crept to his feet
to offer his seat
to the blindlady

people gettingoff
steered carefully around
the black mound
of his back
as they would a pregnantbelly

the littleman
completely unaware
of the embarrassment behind
watched as the blindlady
fingered out her fare

*   *   *

muchlove later he suggested that instead
ofa wedding-cake they should have a miniaturebus
made out of icing but she laughed
and said that buses were for travelling in
and not for eating and besides
you cant taste shapes.

You and Your Strange Ways

increasingly oftennow
you reach into your handbag
(the one I bought some xmasses ago)
and bringing forth
a pair of dead cats
skinned and glistening
like the undersides of tongues
or old elastoplasts
sticky with earwigs
you hurl them at my eyes
and laugh cruellongly
why?
even though we have grown older together
and my kisses are little more than functional
i still love you
you and your strange ways

What You Are

you are the cat's paw
among the silence of midnight goldfish

you are the waves
which cover my feet like cold eiderdowns

you are the teddybear (as good as new)
found beside a road accident

you are the lost day
in the life of a child murderer

you are the underwatertree
around which fish swirl like leaves

you are the green
whose depths I cannot fathom

you are the clean sword
that slaughtered the first innocent

you are the blind mirror
before the curtains are drawn back

you are the drop of dew on a petal
before the clouds weep blood

you are the sweetfresh grass that goes sour
and rots beneath children's feet

you are the rubber glove
dreading the surgeon's brutal hand

you are the wind caught on barbedwire
and crying out against war

you are the moth
entangled in a crown of thorns

you are the apple for teacher
left in a damp cloakroom

you are the smallpox injection
glowing on the torchsinger's arm like a swastika

you are the litmus leaves
quivering on the suntan trees

you are the ivy
which muffles my walls

you are the first footprints in the sand
on bankholiday morning

you are the suitcase full of limbs
waiting in a leftluggage office
to be collected like an orphan

you are a derelict canal
where the tincans whistle no tunes

you are the bleakness of winter before the cuckoo
catching its feathers on a thornbush
heralded spring

you are the stillness of Van Gogh
before he painted the yellow vortex of his last sun

you are the still grandeur of the Lusitania
before she tripped over the torpedo
and laid a world war of american dead
at the foot of the blarneystone

you are the distance
between Hiroshima and Calvary
measured in mother's kisses

you are the distance
between the accident and the telephone box
measured in heartbeats

you are the distance
between power and politicians
measured in half-masts

you are the distance
between advertising and neuroses
measured in phallic symbols

you are the distance
between you and me
measured in tears

you are the moment
before the noose clenched its fist
and the innocent man cried: treason

you are the moment
before the warbooks in the public library
turned into frogs and croaked khaki obscenities

you are the moment
before the buildings turned into flesh
and windows closed their eyes

you are the moment
before the railwaystations burst into tears
and the bookstalls picked their noses

you are the moment
before the buspeople turned into teeth
and chewed the inspector
for no other reason than he was doing his duty

you are the moment
before the flowers turned into plastic and melted
in the heat of the burning cities

you are the moment
before the blindman puts on his dark glasses

you are the moment
before the subconscious begged to be left in peace

you are the moment
before the world was made flesh

you are the moment
before the clouds became locomotives
and hurtled headlong into the sun

you are the moment
before the spotlight moving across the darkened stage
like a crab finds the singer

you are the moment
before the seed nestles in the womb

you are the moment
before the clocks had nervous breakdowns
and refused to keep pace with man's madness

you are the moment
before the cattle were herded together like men

you are the moment
before God forgot His lines

you are the moment of pride
before the fiftieth bead

you are the moment
before the poem passed peacefully away at dawn
like a monarch

The Fish

you always were a strange girl now weren't you?
like the midsummernights party we went to
where towards witching
being tired and hot of dancing
we slipped thro' the frenchwindows
and arminarmed across the lawn

pausing at the artificial pond
lying liquidblack and limpid
in the stricttempo air we kissed
when suddenly you began to tremble
and removing one lavender satin glove knelt
and slipped your hand into the slimy mirror

your face was sad as you brought forth
a switching twitching silver fish
which you lay at my feet
and as the quick tick of the grass
gave way to the slow flop of death
stillkneeling you said softly: 'don't die little fish'

then you tookoff your other glove
and we lay sadly and we made love
as the dancers danced slowly
the fish stared coldly
and the moon admired its reflection
in the lilypetalled pond

My Busconductor

My busconductor tells me
he only has one kidney
and that may soon go on strike
through overwork.
Each busticket
takes on now a different shape
and texture.
He holds a ninepenny single
as if it were a rose
and puts the shilling in his bag
as a child into a gasmeter.
His thin lips
have no quips
for fat factorygirls
and he ignores
the drunk who snores
and the oldman who talks to himself
and gets off at the wrong stop.
He goes gently to the bedroom
of the bus
to collect
and watch familiar shops and pubs passby
(perhaps for the last time?)
The sameold streets look different now
more distinct
as through new glasses.
And the sky
was it ever so blue?
And all the time
deepdown in the deserted busshelter of his mind
he thinks about his journey nearly done.
One day he'll clock on and never clock off
or clock off and never clock on.

Discretion

Discretion is the better part of Valerie
(though all of her is nice)
lips as warm as strawberries
eyes as cold as ice
the very best of everything
only will suffice
not for her potatoes
and puddings made of rice

Not for her potatoes
and puddings made of rice
she takes carbohydrates
like God takes advice
a surfeit of ambition
is her particular vice
Valerie fondles lovers
like a mousetrap fondles mice

And though in the morning
she may whisper: 'it was nice'
you can tell by her demeanour
that she keeps her love on ice
but you've lost your hardearned heart
now you'll have to pay the price
for she'll kiss you on the memory
and vanish in a trice

Valerie is corruptible
but known to be discreet
Valerie rides a silver cloud
where once she walked the street.

There's Something Sad

There's something sad
about the glass
with lipstick on its mouth
that's pointed at and given back
to the waitress in disgust

   Like the girl with the hair-lip
      whom
         no one
            wants
               to
                  kiss.

Vinegar

sometimes
i feel like a priest
in a fish & chip queue
quietly thinking
as the vinegar runs through
how nice it would be
to buy supper for two

Head Injury

I do not smile because I am happy.
Because I gurgle I am not content.
I feel in colours, mottled, mainly black.
And the only sound I hear is the sea
Pounding against the white cliffs of my skull.

For seven months I lay in a coma.
Agony.
Darkness.
My screams drowned by the wind
Of my imperceptible breathing.

One morning the wind died down. I awoke.

You are with me now as you are everyday
Seeking some glimmer of recognition
Some sign of recovery. You take my hand.
I try to say: 'I love you.'
Instead I squawk,
Eyes bobbing like dead birds in a watertank.
I try to say: 'Have pity on me, pity on yourself
Put a bullet between the birds.'
Instead I gurgle.
You kiss me then walk out of the room.
I see your back.
I feel a colour coming, mottled, mainly black.

Dreampoem

in a corner of my bedroom
    grew a tree
    a happytree
    my own tree
its leaves were soft
    like flesh
and its birds sang poems for me
then
    without warning
two men
    with understanding smiles
and axes
    made out of forged excuses
came and chopped it down
either   yesterday
    or the day before
i think it was the day before

Goodbat Nightman

God bless all policemen
and fighters of crime,
May thieves go to jail
for a very long time.

They've had a hard day
helping clean up the town,
Now they hang from the mantelpiece
both upside down.

A glass of warm blood
and then straight up the stairs,
Batman and Robin
are saying their prayers.

*   *   *

They've locked all the doors
and they've put out the bat,
Put on their batjamas
(They like doing that)

They've filled their batwater-bottles
made their batbeds,
With two springy battresses
for sleepy batheads.

They're closing red eyes
and they're counting black sheep,
Batman and Robin
are falling asleep.

Motorway

The politicians,
(who are buying huge cars with hobnailed wheels
        the size of merry-go-rounds)
    have a new plan.
    They are going to
    put cobbles
    in our eyesockets
    and pebbles
    in our navels
    and fill us up
    with asphalt
    and lay us
    side by side
so that we can take a more active part
    in the road
    to destruction.

Icarus Allsorts

*'A meteorite is reported to have landed
in New England. No damage is said . . .'*

A littlebit of heaven fell
From out the sky one day
It landed in the ocean
Not so very far away
The General at the radar screen
Rubbed his hands with glee
And grinning pressed the button
That started World War Three.

From every corner of the earth
Bombs began to fly
There were even missile jams
No traffic lights in the sky
In the times it takes to blow your nose
The people fell, the mushrooms rose

'House!' cried the fatlady
As the bingohall moved to various parts
of the town

'Raus!' cried the German butcher
as his shop came tumbling down

Philip was in the countinghouse
Counting out his money
The Queen was in the parlour
Eating bread and honey
When through the window
Flew a bomb
And made them go all funny

In the time it takes to draw a breath
Or eat a toadstool, instant death

The rich
Huddled outside the doors of their fallout shelters
Like drunken carolsingers

The poor
Clutching shattered televisions
And last week's editions of T.V. Times
(but the very last)

Civil defence volunteers
With their tin hats in one hand
And their heads in the other

C.N.D. supporters
Their ban the bomb badges beginning to rust
Have scrawled 'I told you so' in the dust.

A littlebit of heaven fell
From out the sky one day
It landed in Vermont
North-Eastern U.S.A.
The general at the radar screen
He should have got the sack
But that wouldn't bring
Three thousand million, seven hundred, and sixty-eight
     people back,
Would it?

At Lunchtime

When the bus stopped suddenly to avoid
damaging a mother and child in the road,
the younglady in the green hat sitting opposite
was thrown across me, and not being one
to miss an opportunity i started to make love.

At first she resisted, saying it was too early
in the morning and too soon after breakfast,
and anyway, she found me repulsive.
But when i explained that this being a nuclearage
the world was going to end at lunchtime,
she took off her green hat, put her busticket
into her pocket and joined in the exercise.

The buspeople, and there were many of them,
were shockedandsurprised and amusedandannoyed.
But when word got around that the world
was going to end at lunchtime, they put their pride
in their pockets with their bustickets and made love
one with the other. And even the busconductor,
feeling left out, climbed into the cab
and struck up some sort of relationship with the driver.

That night, on the bus coming home
we were all a little embarrassed,
especially me and the younglady in the green hat,
and we all started to say in different ways
how hasty and foolish we had been.
But then, always having been a bitofalad, i stood up
and said it was a pity that the world didn't nearly end
every lunchtime, and that we could always pretend.
And then it happened . . .

Quick asa crash we all changed partners,
and soon the bus was aquiver
with white, mothball bodies doing naughty things.

And the next day
And everyday
In every bus
In every street
In every town
In every country

People pretended that the world was coming
to an end at lunchtime. It still hasn't.
Although in a way it has.

Mother the Wardrobe is Full of Infantrymen

mother the wardrobe is full of infantrymen
i did i asked them
but they snarled saying it was a mans life

mother there is a centurian tank in the parlour
i did i asked the officer
but he laughed saying 'Queens regulations'
(piano was out of tune anyway)

mother polish your identity bracelet
there is a mushroom cloud in the backgarden
i did it tried to bring in the cat
but it simply came to pieces in my hand
i did i tried to whitewash the windows
but there weren't any
i did i tried to hide under the stairs
but i couldn't get in for civil defence leaders
i did i tried ringing candid camera
but they crossed their hearts

i went for a policeman but they were looting the town
i went out for a fire engine but they were all upside down
i went for a priest but they were all on their knees
mother don't just lie there say something please
mother don't just lie there say something please

Let Me Die a Youngman's Death

Let me die a youngman's death
not a clean & inbetween
the sheets holywater death
not a famous-last-words
peaceful out of breath death

When I'm 73
& in constant good tumour
may I be mown down at dawn
by a bright red sports car
on my way home
from an allnight party

Or when I'm 91
with silver hair
& sitting in a barber's chair
may rival gangsters
with hamfisted tommyguns burst in
& give me a short back & insides

Or when I'm 104
& banned from the Cavern
may my mistress
catching me in bed with her daughter
& fearing for her son
cut me up into little pieces
& throw away every piece but one

Let me die a youngman's death
not a free from sin tiptoe in
candle wax & waning death
not a curtains drawn by angels borne
'what a nice way to go' death

Extracts from *Summer with Monika*

I

they say the sun shone now and again
but it was generally cloudy
with far too much rain

they say babies were born
married couples made love
(often with eachother)
and people died
(sometimes violently)

they say it was an average
              ordinary
              moderate
              run of the mill
              commonorgarden
              summer
. . . but it wasn't

for i locked a yellowdoor
and i threw away the key
and i spent summer with monika
and monika spent summer with me

unlike everybody else
we made friends with the weather . . .
mostdays the sun called
              and sprawled
allover the place

or the wind blew in
as breezily as ever
and ran its fingers through our hair
but usually
it was the moon that kept us company

somedays we thought about the seaside
and built sandcastles on the blankets
and paddled in the pillows
or swam in the sink
and played with the shoals of dishes

otherdays we went for long walks
around the table
and picnicked on the banks
of the settee
or just sunbathed lazily
in front of the fire
until the shilling set on the horizon

we danced a lot that summer . . .
bosanovaed by the bookcase
or maddisoned instead
hulligullied by the oven
or twisted round the bed

at first we kept birds
in a transistor box
to sing for us
but sadly they died
we being too embraced in eachother
to feed them

but it didn't really matter
because we made lovesongs with our bodies
i became the words
and she put me to music

they say it was just
                    like
                    anyother
                    summer
                . . . but it wasn't
for we had love and eachother
and the moon for company
when i spent summer with monika
and
        monika
            spent summer
                with me

2

ten milk bottles standing in the hall
ten milk bottles up against the wall
next door neighbour thinks we're dead
hasnt heard a sound he said
doesnt know weve been in bed
the ten whole days since we were wed

noone knows and noone sees
we lovers doing as we please
but people stop and point at these
ten milk bottles a-turning into cheese

ten milk bottles standing day and night
ten different thicknesses and
different shades of white
persistent carolsingers without a note to utter
silent carolsingers a-turning into butter

now she's run out of passion
and theres not much left in me
so maybe we'll get up
and make a cup of tea
then people can stop wondering
what they're waiting for
those ten milk bottles a-queuing at our door
those ten milk bottles a-queuing at our door

9

i have lately learned to swim
and now feel more at home
in the ebb and flow of your slim
rhythmic tide
than in the fullydressed
        couldntcareless
restless world outside

12

you squeeze my hand and
   cry alittle
you cannot comprehend the
   raggletaggle of living
and think it unfair that
   Death
should be the only one
who knows what he's doing

19

away from you
i feel a great emptiness
a gnawing loneliness

with you
i get that reassuring feeling
of wanting to escape

27

your finger
sadly
has a familiar ring
about it

41

monika the teathings are taking over!
the cups are as big as bubblecars
they throttle round the room
tinopeners skate on the greasy plates
by the light of the silvery moon
the biscuits are having a party
they're necking in our breadbin
thats jazz you hear from the saltcellars
but they don't let nonmembers in
the eggspoons had our eggs for breakfast
the saucebottle's asleep in our bed
i overheard the knives and forks
'it won't be long' they said
'it won't be long' they said.

43

in october
when winter the lodger the sod
came a-knocking at our door
i set in a store
of biscuits and whisky
you filled the hotwaterbottle with tears
and we went to bed until spring

in april
we arose
warm and smelling of morning
we kissed the sleep from eachothers eyes
and went out into the world

and now summer's here again
regular as the rentman
but our lives are now more ordered more arranged
the kissing wildly carefree times have changed

we nolonger stroll along the beaches of the bed
or snuggle in the longgrass of the carpets
the room nolonger a world for makebelieving in
but a ceiling and four walls that are for living in

we nolonger eat our dinner holding hands
or neck in the backstalls of the television
the room nolonger a place for hideandseeking in
but a container that we use for eatandsleeping in

our love has become
                              as comfortable
as the jeans you lounge about in
as my old green coat

                              as necessary
as the change you get from the milkman
for a five pound note
our love has become
                              as nice
as a cup of tea in bed
                              as simple
as something the baby said

monika
            the sky is blue
            the leaves are green
            the birds are singing
            the bells are ringing
            for me and my gal
            the suns as big as an icecream factory
            and the corn is as high as an elephant's
i could go on for hours about the beautiful
weather we're having but monika
            they dont
            make summers
            like they
            used to . . .

BRIAN PATTEN

Somewhere Between Heaven and Woolworths, A Song

She keeps kingfishers in their cages
And goldfish in their bowls,
She is lovely and is afraid
Of such things as growing cold.

She's had enough men to please her,
Though they were more cruel than kind
And their love an act in isolation,
A form of pantomime.

She says she has forgotten
The feelings that she shared
At various all-night parties
Among the couples on the stairs,

For among the songs and dancing
She was once open wide,
A girl dressed in denim
With the boys dressed in lies.

She's eating roses on toast with tulip butter;
Praying for her mirror to stay young;
Though on its no longer gilted surface
This message she has scrawled:

'O somewhere between Heaven and Woolworths
I live I love I scold,
I keep kingfishers in their cages
And goldfish in their bowls.'

Little Johnny's Confession

This morning
      being rather young and foolish
      I borrowed a machinegun my father
      had left hidden since the war, went out,
      and eliminated a number of small enemies.
      Since then I have not returned home.

This morning
      swarms of police with trackerdogs
      wander about the city
      with my description printed
      on their minds, asking:
      'Have you seen him,
      he is seven years old,
      likes Pluto, Mighty Mouse
      and Biffo The Bear,
      have you seen him, anywhere?'

This morning
      sitting alone in a strange playground,
      muttering Youve blundered Youve blundered
      over and over to myself
      I work out my next move
      but cannot move.
      The trackerdogs will sniff me out,
      they have my lollypops.

Party Piece

    He said
'Let's stay here
Now this place has emptied
& make gentle pornography with one another,
While the partygoers go out
& the dawn creeps in,
Like a stranger.

Let us not hesitate
Over what we know
Or over how cold this place has become,
But let's unclip our minds
And let tumble free
The mad, mangled crocodiles of love.'

So they did,
Right there among the woodbines and guinness stains,
And later he caught a bus and she a train
And all there was between them then
was rain.

A Creature to Tell the Time By

I created for myself
a creature to tell the time by
    – & on the lawns of her tongue
flowers grew,
    sweet scented words fell
out her mouth,
her eyes and paws as well were comforting –
    & woken with her
    at dawn, with living birds
humming, alien
inside my head,
I noticed inside us both
the green love that grew there yesterday
    was dead.

Where Are You Now, Batman?

Where are you now, Batman? Now that Aunt Heriot has
        reported Robin missing
And Superman's fallen asleep in the sixpenny childhood
        seats?
Where are you now that Captain Marvel's SHAZAM! echoes
        round the auditorium,
The magicians don't hear it,
Must all be deaf . . . or dead . . .
The Purple Monster who came down from the Purple Planet
        disguised as a man
Is wandering aimlessly about the streets
With no way of getting back,
Sir Galahad's been strangled by the Incredible Living Trees,
Zorro killed by his own sword.
Blackhawk has buried the last of his companions
And has now gone off to commit suicide in the disused
        Hangars of Innocence.
The Monster and the Ape still fight it out in a room
Where the walls are continually closing;
Rocketman's fuel tanks gave out over London.
Even Flash Gordon's lost, podgy and helpless
He wanders among the stars
Weeping over the robots he loved
   Half a universe ago.
                My celluloid companions, it's only a few
                years
Since first I knew you. Yet something in us has already faded.
Has the Terrible Fiend, That Ghastly Adversary,
Mr Old Age, caught you in his deadly trap,
And come finally to polish you off,
His machinegun dripping with years . . .?

A Green Sportscar

(for Mal Doft, racedriver)

. . . And later, to come across
those couples in gleaming green sportscars,
riveted with steel and sprinkled with dawn;
and, still shaking in tarpaulin hoods, the rain
spills onto their faces
as the daylight exposes their E-type deaths.

. . . And later still, to discover
inside him, something has been moved:
She stretched out across him, breasts
pointing towards dawn, who found her last kick
in the sound of the skid on tarmac
of the green-steel coffin in its quiet field.

. . . And finally, to understand them;
they who having been switched off permanently,
are so very still. You would think them asleep,
not dead, if not for the evidence, their expressions
caught at dawn; and held tight beneath
this accidental incident.

Doubt Shall Not Make an End of You

Doubt shall not make an end of you
nor closing eyes lose your shape
when the retina's light fades;
what dawns inside me will light you.

In our public lives we may confine ourselves to darkness,
our nowhere mouths explain away our dreams,
but alone we are incorruptible creatures,
our light sunk too deep to be of any social use
we wander free and perfect without moving

or love on hard carpets
where couples revolving round the room
end found at its centre.

Our love like a whale from its deepest ocean rises –

I offer this and a multitude of images
from party rooms to oceans,
the single star and all its reflections;
being completed we include all
and nothing wishes to escape us.

Beneath my hand your hardening breast agrees
to sing of its own nature,
then from a place without names our origin comes shivering.

Feel nothing separate then,
we have translated each other into light
and into love go streaming.

After Breakfast

After breakfast,
Which is usually coffee and a view
Of teeming rain and the Cathedral old and grey but
Smelling good with grass and ferns
I go out thinking of all those people who've come into this
room
And have slept here
Sad and naked
Alone in pairs
Who came together and
Were they young and white with
Some hint of innocence?
Or did they come simply to come,
To fumble then finally tumble apart,
Or, were they older still, past sex,
Lost in mirrors, contemplating their decay and
What did the morning mean to them?

Perhaps once this room was the servants quarter.
Was she young with freckles, with apple breasts?
Did she ever laugh?
Tease the manservant with her 19th Century charms
And her skirts whirling?
Did she look out through the skylight
And wish she were free, and
What did she have for breakfast?

Waking this morning I think
How good it would be to have someone to share breakfast
with.
Whole families waking!
A thousand negligees, pyjamas, nightgowns
All wandering down to breakfast

How secure! and
Other coming out the far end of dawn
Having only pain and drizzle for breakfast,
Waking always to be greeted with the poor feast of daylight.

How many half lives
Sulking behind these windows
From basement to attic
Complaining and asking
Who will inherit me today?
Who will I share breakfast with?
And always the same answer coming back –

The rain will inherit you – lonely breakfaster!

Song for Last Year's Wife

Alice, this is my first winter
of waking without you, of knowing
that you, dressed in familiar clothes
are elsewhere, perhaps not even
conscious of our anniversary. Have
you noticed? The earth's still as hard,
the same empty gardens exist; it is
as if nothing special had changed,
I wake with another mouth feeding
from me, yet still feel as if
Love had not the right
to walk out of me. A year now. So
what? you say. I send out my spies.
to discover what you are doing. They smile,
return, tell me your body's as firm,
you are as alive, as warm and inviting
as when I knew you first . . . Perhaps it is
the winter, its isolation from other seasons,
that sends me your ghost to witness
when I wake, Somebody came here today, asked
how you were keeping, what
you were doing. I imagine you,
waking in another city, touched
by this same hour. So ordinary
a thing as loss comes now and touches me.

Prosepoem Towards a Definition of Itself

One

When in public poetry should take off its clothes and wave to the nearest person in sight; it should be seen in the company of thieves and lovers rather than that of journalists and publishers. On sighting mathematicians it should unhook the algebra from their minds and replace it with poetry; on sighting poets it should unhook poetry from their minds and replace it with algebra; it should fall in love with children and woo them with fairytales; it should wait on the landing for 2 years for its mates to come home then go outside and find them all dead.

When the electricity fails it should wear dark glasses and pretend to be blind. It should guide all those who are safe into the middle of busy roads and leave them there. It should scatter woodworm into the bedrooms of all peg-legged men not being afraid to hurt the innocent. It should shout EVIL! EVIL! from the roofs of the world's stock exchanges. It should not pretend to be a clerk or a librarian. It should be kind, it is the eventual sameness of contradictions. It should never weep until it is alone and then only after it has covered the mirrors and sealed up the cracks.

Poetry should seek out pale and lyrical couples and wander with them into stables, neglected bedrooms and engineless cars for a final Good Time. It should enter burning factories too late to save anyone. It should pay no attention to its real name.

Poetry should be seen lying by the side of road accidents, hissing from unlit gasrings. It should scrawl the nymphomaniac's secret on her teacher's blackboard; offer her a worm saying: Inside this is a tiny apple. Poetry should play hopscotch in the 6pm streets and look for jinks in other people's dustbins. At dawn it should leave the bedroom and catch the first bus home to its wife. At dusk it should

chatup a girl nobody wants. It should be seen standing on the ledge
of a skyscraper, on a bridge with a brick tied around its heart.
It is the monster hiding in a child's dark room, it is the scar on a
beautiful man's face. It is the last blade of grass being picked from
the city park.

Two

The Obsolete Nightingale

When long ago it became apparent that the lion
had no intentions of lyring down with the lamb
you, still believing in that obsolete fable,
were thrown into chaos.

From somewhere inside you
time and again you dragged out the lamb,
and inviting the lion in from the nervous world
put the fable to the test.

Each night through the walls the slaughter leaked,
your neighbours became addicted.

A terminal romantic, a confused source-seeker,
in the bedrooms of cheap hotels you open your suitcase,
and unfolding the soiled rainbows
sleep among them.

Poetry is the interval during which nothing is said,
the sign-board on which nothing is written.
It is the astronaut stepping from the first time into liquid
       space.
It follows its imagination out across the frozen lakes,
out to where the small footprints have ended.

It is the surgeon cutting deeper and deeper,
bewildered by the depths.
It sings for the children who keep clouds in their pockets,
for the midwives tasting of grass,
for the impending dust,
for the card-dealers who pull out the Milky Way
as a last resort.

At the festival of fools it erects a bedraggled maypole
and dances to a music of its own invention.

In the conference rooms where the great minds gather
where the politicians squark
and the philosophers brood
it serves the drinks,
in the halls where the fashionable dance
it robs the overcoats.

It stands in red kiosks exhausting
the phone books of generations.
It is the acceptable lie in a time
of acceptable lies.

*   *   *

When the professor of literature steps into the shadow of a
        lectern
and when the students are finally seated
and the whispers have died away
poetry puts on an overcoat
and sick of threadbare souls,
steps out into the streets weeping.

It is the clue overlooked by policemen;
the stranger walking through the airport terminal;
the blue egg found crushed in a nest.

It is the address thrown from the window
of a passing train.
I sit in motorway cafes staring through windows.
You are there,
running across the wet fields,
the logicians howling after you.

They have given the hounds platefuls of roses,
stuffed their noses with tulips –
they'll give you no rest, poetry.
From the roofs of articulate houses
the scholars will snipe at you.

It is rumoured one among them
has transmuted gold into dust.

I have found you among strangers,
among faces that pick about in time,
choosing the length of their days
and the length of their suffering.

I have found you most often in sadness,
on evenings when each patch of ground
seems remote as an island,
when rooms are bleakest and speech is incoherent,
when words choke,
fish thrown up from the paranoiac pools.

You belong to these generations drifting between buildings,
unlovely mammals, pale as worms,
lamenting their own temporariness.

You are the chameleon crawling across rainbows.

And I am anchored among your contradictions:
Wrapped in obsolete kindness,
too caring in days ruled by slaughter,
too gentle among the truncheons and the nights fed on
    disaster

you wander about the city whispering
'Where's the bloodbath this evening?'
'What new mutilations are available?'
You wander through each face looking for the one
that will best mirror your own.
The list of your affairs is endless.

*　　　*　　　*

Poetry asks the head-office for its files on the nightingale,
for all information regarding its colour,
its shape, the kind of song it indulged in.
The message comes back:
'Subject obsolete. File closed.'

6.15 am　Across the Thames busloads of charladies wander
gossiping about disease;
truckloads of bleached meat are unloaded in front of
　　　futuristic towers.

Worn faces, faded print dresses,
exhausted overcoats,
all refusing to announce the daylight as miracle.

The Embankment is thick with rain,
with cardboard boxes in which dignity flounders.
From the river poetry fishes out an image
of a dead bird floating beneath vanished starlight.

It is the same old story.
Night owns the copyright.

And always there will be the dream of travelling,
of boarding the boats sailing from trivia,
And always there will be the regret,
the sense of carnivals finished.

Poetry, what of your education? Your vocabulary was limited, you
studied impossibilities wrote essays on impatience that were never
finished, you stared at the atlas, invented journeys you were too

young to set out upon. You planned meetings with alien invaders, in the school laboratories you invented a cure for obedience. Were you hidden, disguised as frost on the spiky railings of schoolyards? Time and again I have gone to you for advice and searching through pages of unremarkable confessions have found among the heart's trash nothing but revelations. It is the mirror in front of which the years tremble, it is the laughter borrowed momentarily from strangers. It is the final sentence, echoing forever.

Something That Was Not There Before

Something that was not there before
has come through the mirror
into my room.

It is not such a simple creature
as at first I thought –
from somewhere it has brought a mischief

that troubles both silence and objects,
and now left alone here
I weave intricate reasons for its arrival.

They disintegrate. Today in January, with
the light frozen on my window, I hear outside
a million panicking birds, and know even out there

comfort is done with; it has shattered
even the stars, this creature
at last come home to me.

In a New Kind of Dawn

In a new kind of dawn
readjusting your conscience
you wake, and

woken you dream
or so it seems
of the forests you've come across

& lives you'd have swum in
had you been strong enough.

On the Dawn Boat

on the dawn boat,
coming awake,
the land empty, I thought

about it, about
the many warnings,
the many signs, but

none to lead me
away from here, none
to lead me there.

Interruption at the Opera House

At the very beginning of an important symphony,
while the rich and famous were settling into their quietly
    expensive boxes,

a man came crashing through the crowds,
carrying in his hand a cage in which
the rightful owner of the music sat,
yellow and tiny and very poor;
and taking onto the rostrum this rather timid bird
he turned up the microphone, and it sang.

'A very original beginning to the evening,' said the crowds,
quietly glancing at their programmes to find
the significance of the intrusion.

Meanwhile at the box office, the organizers of the evening
were arranging for small and uniformed attendants
to evict, even forcefully, the intruders.
But as the attendants, poor and gathered from the nearby
    slums at little expense,
went rushing down the aisles to do their job
they heard, above the coughing and irritable rattle of jewels,
a sound that filled their heads with light,
and from somewhere inside them there bubbled up a stream,
and there came a breeze on which their youth was carried.
How sweetly the bird sang!
And though soon the fur-wrapped crowds
were leaving their boxes and in confusion were winding their
    way home
still the attendants sat in the aisles,
and some, so delighted at what they heard, rushed out to call
their families and friends.

And their children came,
sleepy for it was late in the evening,
very late in the evening,
and they hardly knew if they had done with dreaming
or had begun again.

In all the tenement blocks
the lights were clicking on,
and the rightful owner of the music,
tiny but no longer timid, sang
for the rightful owners of the song.

A Small Dragon

I've found a small dragon in the woodshed.
Think it must have come from deep inside a forest
because it's damp and green and leaves
are still reflecting in its eyes.

I fed it on many things, tried grass,
the roots of stars, hazel-nut and dandelion,
but it stared up at me as if to say, I need
foods you can't provide.

It made a nest among the coal,
not unlike a bird's but larger.
It is out of place here
and is quite silent.

If you believed in it I would come
hurrying to your house to let you share my wonder,
but I want instead to see
if you yourself will pass this way.

Sing Softly

Sing softly
now sadly
of rains he has known,

of dawns when
his visions
were of damp boys

slim and brown,
walking at the edge
of cold rivers.

O they were
the palest of children,
stripping.

Slim fish
darting through water,
laughing now and then.

Sleep Now

(In Memory of Wilfred Owen)

Sleep now,
Your blood moving in the quiet wind;
No longer afraid of the rabbits
Hurrying through the tall grass
Or the faces laughing on the beach
And among the cold trees.

Sleep now,
Alone in the sleeves of grief,
Listening to clothes falling
And to your flesh touching God;
To the chatter and backslapping
Of Christ meeting heroes of war.

Sleep now,
Your words have passed
The lights shining from the East
And the sound of the flack
Raping graves and emptying seasons.

You do not hear the dry wind pray
Or the children play
A game called 'Soldiers' in the street.

Seascape

gulls kiss the sun
and you walk on the beach
afraid of the tide

from the sea's warm belly
a lobster crawls to
see if we've gone

but mouths still talk
and finding out my lips
I say to you:

'lie silently
and stretch out your arms
like seaweed strangled by the wind'

out of a seashell
a sandcrab pokes his head
and sniffs the salt wind

now afraid we sit in silence
and watching the sun go down
I ask you your name

The River Arse

The rain is teeming
    across the river
falling on the arse of
    a nude girl swimming
without even a splash
    & O it's such a pretty little arse
see how it rises now and then
    like an island
a pink island moving through the water
    something young and good
in the river that flows out of Lyons
    a nude arse and a special one at that
belonging to a swimmer floating
    in the opposite direction
to the shore.

Meat

Some pretty little thoughts,
some wise little songs,
some neatly packed observations,
some descriptions of peacocks, of sunsets,
some fat little tears,
something to hold to chubby breasts,
something to put down,
something to sigh about,
I don't want to give you these things.
I want to give you meat,
the splendid meat,
the blemished meat.
Say, here it is,
here is the active ingredient,
the thing that bothers history,
that bothers priest and financier.
Here is the meat.
The sirens wailing on police-cars,
the ambulances alert with pain,
the bricks falling on the young
queens in night-parks
demand meat, the real thing.
I want to give you something
that bleeds as it leaves my hand
and enters yours,
something that by its rawness,
that by its bleeding
demands to be called real.

In the morning, when you wake,
the sheets are blood-soaked.
For no apparent reason
they're soaked in blood.

Here is the evidence you have been waiting for.
Here is the minor revelation.

A fly made out of meat lands
on a wall made out of meat.
There is meat in the pillows we lie on.
The eiderdowns are full of meat.
I want to give it you
share the headache of the doctor
bending irritated by the beds
as he deals out the hushed truth about the meat,
the meat that can't be saved,
that's got to end,
that's going to be tossed away.

At night the meat rocks between sheets
butchered by its own longings.
You can strip the meat,
you can sit on it,
you can caress and have sex with it –
the thing that carries its pain around,
that's born in pain,
that lives in pain,
that eats itself to keep itself in pain.

My neighbours driving away in their cars
are moody and quiet and do not talk to me.
I want to fill their cars with meat,
stuff it down their televisions,
leave it in the laundromat
where the shy secretaries gather.

At the fashionable parties the fashionable meat dances,
Studded with jewelry it dances,
How delicately it holds its wine glasses,
How intelligently it discusses
The latest mass-butchering!

Repetitive among the petals,
among the songs repetitive,
I want the stuff to breathe its name,
the artery to open up and whisper,
I am the meat,
the sole inventor of paradise.
I am the thing denied entrance into heaven,
awkward and perishable,
the most neglected of mammals.
I am the meat that glitters,
that weeps over its temporariness.

I want the furniture to turn into meat,
the door handle as you touch it
to change into meat.
The meat you are shy to take home to mother,
the meat you are,
gone fat and awkward.
Hang it above your bed,
in the morning when you wake drowsy
find it in the wash-basin.
Nail it to the front door.
In the evening leave it out on the lawns.
The meat that thinks the stars are white flies.

Let the dawn traveller find it among hedgerows,
waiting to offer itself as he passes.
Leave it out among the night-patrols and the lovers.
Leave it between the memorandums of politicians.
Here is the active ingredient;
here is the thing that bothers history,
that bothers priest and financier.
Pimply and blunt and white,
it comes towards you with its arms outstretched.
How you love the meat!

Room

Room you're toneless now.
Room you don't belong to me
I want another room I want one
without your tattymemories
I want to brush you out into the streets where
you'll become a debris full of children's laughter
Room you're murderous
You're a crooked woman with armpits full of lice
You're no good to me
You make me feel like an accident
Make me blush with your crude jokes
and your old iron bedsteads
Room you've made me weep too many times
I'm sick of you and all your faces
I go into houses and find its still you only this time
you're wearing a different disguise
I send out my spies to find who you're living with
but they don't return
I send myself out and find you eating my spies.
Its impossible. You stand there dusty and naked
Your records spinning mutely
Your head vomiting up bodies
Your books all empty
Your gasstoves hissing
Wallpaper crying sighing it doesn't matter
for your windows have become taperecordings of the night
and only death will shove you to sleep.
I'm going to leave you
Going to spend all my dreams
Once in you I could lie and hear the spyingmoon apologize
as it tiptoed through the clouds

and left you in your special darkness
But its different now, now
only the rain splatters through
and the one other sound is you whispering
'I'm not around you I'm in you all my walls are in you'
Room you're full of my own graves!

Come into the City, Maud

'Come in to the garden, Maud,
For the black bat, night, has flown.'
  – Tennyson

Maud, where are you Maud?
With your long dresses and peachcream complexion;
In what cage did you hang that black bat night?
What took place in the garden? Maud, it is over,
You can tell us now.

Still lyrical but much used, you wander about the suburbs
Watching the buses go past full of young happy people,
Wondering where the garden is, wherever can it be,
And how can it be lost. Maud, it's no use.

Can it be that you got yourself lost
And are living with an out of work musician,
You share a furnished room and have an old wireless
That tells you the latest bad news.
What's happening Maud?

Do you wear a Mary Quant dress
And eat fish and chips alone at night?
Wear make-up that tastes of forget-me-nots?
Where are you? and are you very lost,
Very much alone?
Do you cry for that garden, lost among pornographic
    suggestions,
Where the concrete flowers neither open nor close;
Who poured weedkiller over your innocence?

We could not find that garden for you,
Even if we tried.

So, come into the city Maud,
Where the flowers are too quickly picked
And the days are butchered as if they were enemies.

Maud, is that you I see
Alone among the office blocks,
Head bowed, young tears singing pop-sorrow
On your cheeks?

Schoolboy

Before playtime let us consider the possibilities
of getting stoned on milk.

    In his dreams,
scribbling overcharged on woodbines,
mumbling obscure sentences into his desk
'No way of getting out,
no way out . . .'
                Poet dying of
too much education, school bullies, examinations,
canes that walk the nurseries of his wet dreams;
satchels full of chewing gum, bad jokes, pencils;
crude drawings performed in the name of art. Soon will
come the Joyful Realization in Mary's back kitchen
      while mother's out.
All this during chemistry.

(The headmaster's crying in his study.
His old pinstriped pants rolled up to his knees
in a vain attempt to recapture youth; emotions
skid along his slippery age; Love, smeared across his face,
like a road accident.)

The schoolyard's full of people to hate.
Full of tick and prefects and a fat schoolmaster
and whistles and older and younger boys, but
he's growing sadly,
   sadly
      growing
         up.

Girls,
   becoming mysterious, are now more important
than arriving at school late or receiving trival awards.
Photographs of those huge women
                seem a little more believable now.

(Secretly, the pale, unmarried headmaster telling him
Death is the only grammatically correct full-
                            stop.)

Girls,
   still mysterious;
arithmetic thighed, breasts measured in thumbprints,
not inches.
Literature's just another way out.
History's full of absurd mistakes.
King Arthur if he ever existed
would only have farted and excused himself
from the Round Table in a hurry.

(The headmaster, staring through the study window
into the playground, composes evil poems about
the lyrical boy in class four)
              'He invited us up sir,
           but not for the cane,
              said the algebra of life
                  was too difficult to explain
                     and that all equations
                        mounted to nothing . . .'

Growing up's wonderful if
            you keep your eyes
                closed tightly, and
if you manage to grow
            take your soul with you,
                nobody wants it.

So,
playtime's finished with;
It's time to fathom out too many things:
To learn he's got a different authority watching over him.
The teacher gives way to the police,
Detention gives way to the prison.

He's going to learn strange things, learn
how to lie correctly, how to cheat and steal
        (in the nicest possible manner).
He will learn, amongst other things, how to enjoy
his enemies, how to avoid friendships. If he's unlucky
he will learn how to love and give everything away,
and how eventually he'll end up with nothing.

        Between himself and the grave
            his parents stand,
                monuments that will crumble.

        He won't understand many things.
He'll just accept them. He'll experiment with hardboiled
            eggs all his life
and die a stranger in a race attempting Humanity.

        And finally,
the playground full of dust,
        crates of sour milk lining the corridors;
            the headmaster, weeping quietly among the saws and
                                            chisels
            in the damp woodwork room;

        The ghosts of Tim and Maureen and Patrick
            and Nancy and so many others,
        all confused with sexual longings, all
                doomed to living, and

one pale boy
in a steamy room
looking outside across the roofs and chimneys
where it seems, the clouds are crying,
where ambitions are marked 'perishable',
where the daylight's gone blind
and his teachers, all dead.

On a Horse Called Autumn

(for Maureen)

On a horse called autumn
among certain decaying things
she rides inside me, for

no matter where I move
this puzzled woman sings
of nude horsemen, breeched
in leather,

of stables decaying near
where once
riders came,

and where now along
her heart journeys, among
lies I made real.

Now riding in truth
what alterations can I make
knowing nothing will change?

Things stay the same:
such journeys as hers
are the ones I care for.

Ode on Celestial Music

(or, It's The Girl in the Bathroom Singing)

It's not celestial music,
it's the girl downstairs in the bathroom singing.
You can tell. Although it's winter
the trees outside her window have grown leaves,
all manner of flowers push up through the floorboards.
I think – what a filthy trick that is to play on me,
I snip them with my scissors shouting
'I want only bona fide celestial music!'
Hearing this she stops singing.

Out of her bath now the girl knocks on my door.
'Is my singing disturbing you?' she smiles entering.
'Did you say it was licentious or sensual?
And excuse me, my bath towel's slipping.'
A warm and blonde creature.
I slam the door on her breasts shouting
'I want only bona fide celestial music!'

Much later on in life I wear my hearing aid.
What have I done to my body, ignoring it,
splitting things into so many pieces my hands
cannot mend anything? The stars, the buggers, remained
      silent.
Down in the bathroom now her daughter is singing.
Turning my hearing aid full volume
I bend close to the floorboards hoping
for at least one song to get through.

A Talk with a Wood

Moving through you one evening
when you offered shelter to
quiet things soaked in rain

I saw through your thinning branches
the beginnings of suburbs, and
frightened by the rain,

grey hares running upright in
distant fields; and quite alone there
I thought of nothing but my footprints

being filled, and love, distilled
of people, drifted free, then
the woods spoke with me.

Travelling Between Places

Leaving nothing and nothing ahead;
when you stop for the evening
the sky will be in ruins,

when you hear late birds
with tired throats singing
think how good it is that they,

knowing you were coming,
stayed up late to greet you
who travels between places

when the late afternoon
drifts into the woods, when
nothing matters specially.

Looking Back at It

At nineteen I was a Brave Old Hunchback
    Climbing to 'tremendous heights'
Preparing to swing down on my golden rope
    And rescue the Accused Innocence.
But on my swooping, downwards path one day
            Innocence ducked
And I amazed at such an act crashed into
        a wall she had been building,

How silly now to think myself able to rescue anything!

The Last Residents

Mayakovsky, sitting at your window one afternoon,
Half-crazy with sorrow, your soul finally shipwrecked,
What if you had decided to be foolish,
To be neither cynical nor over-serious,
In fact, not to care?

Would Russia have changed much?
The snows melted in Siberia?
The bright posters propagated a different message?
Would the winter birds, numbed in their trees,
Not have fallen?
Would they have re-raised their heads singing?

These years later I sit at a window in London and see
The same events occurring;
Quieter, more subtly now
Are the prisons fed, the warrants issued.
And the end still seems the same,
The outcome as inevitable.

And no matter how much I care,
This song will resolve nothing:
I still see the stars turn negative,
And the last residents of London
Crumble among the plagued allotments
Crying out, crying
With disbelief and absurd astonishment.

Contemporary ... Provocative ... Outrageous ...
Prophetic ... Groundbreaking ... Funny ... Disturbing ...
Different ... Moving ... Revolutionary ... Inspiring ...
Subversive ... Life-changing ...

What makes a modern classic?

At Penguin Classics our mission has always been to make the best
books ever written available to everyone. And that also means
constantly redefining and refreshing exactly what makes a 'classic'.
That's where Modern Classics come in. Since 1961 they have been an
organic, ever-growing and ever-evolving list of books from the last
hundred (or so) years that we believe will continue to be read over and
over again.

They could be books that have inspired political dissent, such as
Animal Farm. Some, like *Lolita* or *A Clockwork Orange*, may have
caused shock and outrage. Many have led to great films, from *In Cold
Blood* to *One Flew Over the Cuckoo's Nest*. They have broken down
barriers – whether social, sexual, or, in the case of *Ulysses*, the
boundaries of language itself. And they might – like *Goldfinger* or
Scoop – just be pure classic escapism. Whatever the reason, Penguin
Modern Classics continue to inspire, entertain and enlighten millions
of readers everywhere.

'No publisher has had more influence on reading habits than Penguin'
Independent

'Penguins provided a crash course in world literature'
Guardian

The best books ever written

PENGUIN ((🐧)) CLASSICS

SINCE 1946

Find out more at www.penguinclassics.com

PENGUIN MODERN CLASSICS

THE MONKEY WRENCH GANG
EDWARD ABBEY

'A man of great passion and love of the natural order' Robert Redford

The construction of the colossal Glen Canyon Dam on the Colorado River spurs an oddball quartet of eco-activists to join forces in a noble cause. A Vietnam veteran who loves booze, guns and the great outdoors, a billboard-burning doctor, a feminist revolutionary and a polygamist riverboat guide – the Monkey Wrench Gang go up against the vultures of big business to sabotage the strip mines, power plants and concrete dams that are destroying vast tracts of the wilderness, through peaceful means – or otherwise …

Scandalizing the establishment and read by others as a call-to-arms when it appeared in 1975, *The Monkey Wrench Gang* is a wildly funny and provocatively satirical book that ignited the flames of environmental activism.

'A terrific read – funny, perceptive, brutally honest, and extremely timely' Eric Schlosser

With a Preface by Robert Redford and an Introduction by Eric Schlosser

PENGUIN MODERN CLASSICS

A MAN OF THE PEOPLE
CHINUA ACHEBE

'A bitter yet funny satire … probably the best book to come out of West Africa'
Anthony Burgess

Chief the Honourable M. A. Nanga, MP jacked in his job as a teacher to become a
politician. As Minister for Culture he is 'a man of the people', as cynical as he is
charming, a roguish opportunist who can talk his way in and out of anything. At
first, the contrast between Nanga and Odili, a former pupil who is visiting the
Ministry, appears huge. But in the 'eat-and-let-eat' atmosphere, Odili's idealism
soon collides with his lusts – and the two mens' personal and political tauntings
threaten to send their country spinning into chaos.

Published, prophetically, just days before Nigeria's first attempted coup in 1966, *A
Man of the People* is Achebe's keen-eyed analysis of post-independence African
politics where, all to easily, men found themselves 'brutalised by circumstance'
and prey to corruption.

Penguin Modern Classics

ANTHILLS OF THE SAVANNAH
CHINUA ACHEBE

'Worshipping a dictator is such a pain in the ass ….'

Chris, Ikem and Beatrice are three like-minded friends working under the military regime of His Excellency, the Sandhurst-educated President of Kangan. In the pressurized atmosphere of oppression and intimidation they are simply trying to live and love – and remain friends. But in a world where each day brings a new betrayal, hope is hard to cling on to.

Achebe's candid vision of contemporary African politics is a powerful fusion of angry voices and flashes of poetry. But his interpretation of post-oil-boom Nigeria is not defeatist; like his character Beatrice, Achebe refuses to disparage the day that still has an hour of light in its hand.

'[The writer] in whose company the prison walls fell down' Nelson Mandela

PENGUIN MODERN CLASSICS

MAPP AND LUCIA
E. F. BENSON

'Enchanting ... even at their worst-behaved, his characters never stop being lovable' Philip Hensher

When the recently widowed Mrs Emmeline Lucas (Lucia to her friends) desires a change of scene, she determines on the picturesque seaside town of Tilling for an extended break. There, with her ever-faithful friend and accomplice Georgie Pillson in tow, she sets forth to wrest the reins of Tilling society from Miss Elizabeth Mapp. But the Machiavellian Lucia has not reckoned on the indomitable Mapp, who has no intention of giving up her supremacy. Has Lucia at last met her match?

Battle-lines are swiftly drawn as the ladies strive to outdo each other, using invitations to delightful garden parties and, above all, the recipe for 'Lobster *à la Riseholme*' as their deadly weapons (to the fascinated horror of their friends), for the position of doyenne of Tilling.

'We will pay anything for Lucia books' Noël Coward, Gertrude Lawrence, Nancy Mitford, W. H. Auden

With an Introduction by Philip Hensher

He just wanted a decent book to read ...

Not too much to ask, is it? It was in 1935 when Allen Lane, Managing Director of Bodley Head Publishers, stood on a platform at Exeter railway station looking for something good to read on his journey back to London. His choice was limited to popular magazines and poor-quality paperbacks – the same choice faced every day by the vast majority of readers, few of whom could afford hardbacks. Lane's disappointment and subsequent anger at the range of books generally available led him to found a company – and change the world.

'We believed in the existence in this country of a vast reading public for intelligent books at a low price, and staked everything on it'
Sir Allen Lane, 1902–1970, founder of Penguin Books

The quality paperback had arrived – and not just in bookshops. Lane was adamant that his Penguins should appear in chain stores and tobacconists, and should cost no more than a packet of cigarettes.

Reading habits (and cigarette prices) have changed since 1935, but Penguin still believes in publishing the best books for everybody to enjoy. We still believe that good design costs no more than bad design, and we still believe that quality books published passionately and responsibly make the world a better place.

So wherever you see the little bird – whether it's on a piece of prize-winning literary fiction or a celebrity autobiography, political tour de force or historical masterpiece, a serial-killer thriller, reference book, world classic or a piece of pure escapism – you can bet that it represents the very best that the genre has to offer.

Whatever you like to read – trust Penguin.